My Air Fryer Cookbook

Tasty and Affordable Air Fryer Recipes to
Start Your Day with the Right Foot

Kira Hamm

TABLE OF CONTENT

this book has been derived from various sources. Please consult a licensed professional before attempting any techniques outlined in this book.

By reading this document, the reader agrees that under no circumstances is the author responsible for any losses, direct or indirect, which are incurred as a result of the use of information contained within this document, including, but not limited to, — errors, omissions, or inaccuracies.

Broccoli Quiche

Preparation Time: 10 minutes

Cooking Time: 10 minutes

Servings: 1

Ingredients:

1 egg

1 tbsp cheddar cheese, grated

4 broccoli florets

3 tbsp heavy cream

Directions:

Spray 5-inch quiche dish with cooking spray.

In a bowl, whisk the egg with cheese, cream, pepper, and salt. Add broccoli and stir well.

Pour egg mixture into the quiche dish.

Place dish into the air fryer basket and cook at 325 F for 10 minutes.

Nutrition: Calories 173 Fat 13 g Carbohydrates 6.5 g Sugar 1.9 g Protein 9.9 g Cholesterol 191 mg

Broccoli Fritters

Preparation Time:10 minutes

Cooking Time: 15 minutes

Servings:4

Ingredients:

3 cups broccoli florets, steam & chopped

2 cups cheddar cheese, shredded

1/4 cup almond flour

2 eggs, lightly beaten

2 garlic cloves, minced

Directions:

Line air fryer basket with parchment paper.

Add all Ingredients into the mixing bowl and mix until well combined.

Make patties from broccoli mixture and place in the air fryer basket.

Cook at 375 F for 15 minutes. Turn patties halfway through.

Nutrition: Calories 285 Fat 22 g Carbohydrates 6.3 g Sugar 1.7 g Protein 19.2 g Cholesterol 141 mg

Spicy Brussels Sprouts

Preparation Time:10 minutes

Cooking Time: 14 minutes

Servings:2

Ingredients:

1/2 lb. Brussels sprouts, trimmed and halved

1 tbsp chives, chopped

1/4 tsp cayenne

1/2 tsp chili powder

1/2 tbsp olive oil

Directions:

Add all Ingredients: into the large bowl and toss well.

Spread Brussels sprouts in the air fryer basket and cook at 370 F for 14 minutes. Shake basket halfway through.

Nutrition: Calories 82 Fat 4.1 g Carbohydrates 10.9 g Sugar 2.6 g Protein 4 g Cholesterol 0 mg

Zucchini Breakfast Patties

Preparation Time:10 minutes

Cooking Time: 15 minutes

Servings:6

Ingredients:

> 1 cup zucchini, shredded and squeeze out all liquid
>
> 2 tbsp onion, minced
>
> 1 egg, lightly beaten
>
> 1/4 tsp red pepper flakes
>
> 1/4 cup parmesan cheese, grated

Directions:

> Add all Ingredients into the bowl and mix until well combined.
>
> Make small patties from the zucchini mixture and place it into the air fryer basket.
>
> Cook at 400 F for 15 minutes.

Nutrition: Calories 48 Fat 3.3 g Carbohydrates 2.1 g Sugar 0.7 g Protein 3.1 g Cholesterol 31 mg

Tasty Herb Egg Cups

Preparation Time:10 minutes

Cooking Time: 20 minutes

Servings:6

Ingredients:

6 eggs

1/2 tbsp chives, chopped

1/2 tbsp fresh dill, chopped

1 tbsp fresh parsley, chopped

1/2 tbsp fresh basil, chopped

1/4 cup mozzarella cheese, grated

Directions:

In a bowl, whisk eggs with pepper and salt. Add remaining ingredients and stir well.

Pour egg mixture into the silicone muffin molds.

Place molds into the air fryer basket and cook at 350 F for 20 minutes.

Nutrition: Calories 67 Fat 4.6 g Carbohydrates 0.6 g Sugar 0.4 g Protein 6 g Cholesterol 164 mg

Veggie Frittata

Preparation Time:10 minutes

Cooking Time: 20 minutes

Servings:2

Ingredients:

    4 eggs

    1 cup bell peppers, chopped

    1 cup zucchini, chopped

    1 cup mushrooms, sliced

    2 tbsp coconut milk

    1 tbsp olive oil

    1 cup cheddar cheese

    1/2 cup onion, chopped

Directions:

Spray air fryer safe pan with cooking spray and set aside.

Heat oil in a medium pan over medium heat. Add onion, bell peppers, zucchini, and mushrooms, and sauté for 5 minutes.

Remove pan from heat and set aside to cool.

In a bowl, whisk eggs with milk, pepper, and salt.

Add sautéed vegetables and cheese and stir
well.

Pour egg mixture into the pan.

Place pan in the air fryer basket and cook at
350 F for 20 minutes.

Nutrition: Calories 495 Fat 38.4 g Carbohydrates
12.5 g Sugar 7.3 g Protein 28.2 g Cholesterol 387
mg

Bell Pepper Broccoli Frittata

Preparation Time:10 minutes

Cooking Time: 17 minutes

Servings:2

Ingredients:

3 eggs

1/2 cup bell pepper, chopped

1/2 cup broccoli florets

2 tbsp parmesan cheese, grated

2 tbsp coconut milk

Directions:

Spray air fryer safe pan with cooking spray and set aside.

Place bell peppers and broccoli in the pan.

Cook broccoli and bell pepper at 350 F for 7 minutes.

In a bowl, whisk together eggs, milk, and seasoning.

Once the vegetable is cooked then pour egg mixture over vegetable and sprinkle cheese on top.

Return pan in the air fryer basket and cook for 10 minutes more.

Nutrition: Calories 191 Fat 13.3 g Carbohydrates 5.6 g Sugar 2.9 g Protein 14.1 g Cholesterol 256 mg

Spinach & Ricotta Cups

Preparation Time:10 m

Cooking Time: 10 m

Servings: 2

Ingredients:

>   2 large eggs
>
>   2 tablespoons heavy cream
>
>   2 tablespoons frozen spinach, thawed
>
>   4 teaspoons ricotta cheese, crumbled
>
>   Salt and freshly ground black pepper, to taste

Directions:

>   Grease 2 ramekins.
>
>   In each ramekin, crack one egg.
>
>   Divide the cream spinach, cheese, salt, and black pepper in each ramekin and gently stir to mix without breaking the yolks.
>
>   Turn the "Temperature Knob" of Power XL Air Fryer Grill to line the temperature to 330 degrees F.
>
>   Turn the "Function Knob" to settle on "Air Fry."
>
>   Turn the "Timer Knob" to line the Time for 10 minutes.

After preheating, arrange the ramekins pan over the roasting rack.

Insert the roasting rack at position 2 of the Air Fryer Grill.

When the cooking Time is over, remove the ramekins and place them onto a wire rack to chill for five minutes before serving.

Nutrition: Calories: 138 Kcal, Fat: 11.4g, Carb: 1.4g, Protein: 7.8g

Mini Spinach Quiches

Preparation Time:10 m

Cooking Time: 25 m

Servings: 6

Ingredients:

> 2 (9-inch) premade pie crusts, thawed
>
> 2 eggs
>
> ½ cup sharp cheddar cheese, shredded
>
> ¼ cup whole milk
>
> ¼ cup heavy cream
>
> ¼ cup frozen spinach, drained
>
> Salt and freshly ground black pepper, to taste

Directions:

> Arrange the circles into a 6 cups muffin pan.
>
> With a fork, holes in the bottom of every pie shell and put aside.
>
> In a bowl, add the remaining ingredients and beat until well combined.
>
> Divide the mixture over each pie shell evenly.
>
> Turn the "Temperature Knob" of Power XL Air Fryer Grill to line the temperature to 375 degrees F.
>
> Turn the "Function Knob" to settle on "Bake."

Turn the "Timer Knob" to line the Time for 25 minutes.

After preheating, arrange the muffin pan over the roasting rack.

Insert the roasting rack at position 3 of the Air Fryer Grill.

When the cooking Time is over, remove the muffin pan and put it aside for about 5 minutes before serving.

Nutrition: Calories: 329 Kcal, Fat: 22g, Carb: 23.2g, Protein: 7.7g

Mushroom Cheese Egg Bake

Preparation Time:10 minutes

Cooking Time: 8 minutes

Servings:1

Ingredients:

2 eggs

1/2 cup ham, diced

1/4 cup cheddar cheese, shredded

1/4 cup coconut milk

2 mushrooms, sliced

1 tbsp green onion, chopped

Directions:

Spray air fryer safe pan with cooking spray and set aside.

In a bowl, whisk eggs with cheese, milk, pepper, and salt. Add ham, mushrooms, and green onion and stir well.

Pour egg mixture into the pan.

Place pan into the air fryer basket and cook at 330 F for 8 minutes.

Nutrition: Calories 498 Fat 38.3 g Carbohydrates 8.6 g Sugar 3.6 g Protein 31.9 g Cholesterol 396 mg

Breakfast Radish Hash Browns

Preparation Time:10 minutes

Cooking Time: 13 minutes

Servings:2

Ingredients:

1 lb. radishes, clean and sliced

1 onion, sliced

1 tbsp olive oil

1 tsp onion powder

1 tsp garlic powder

1/2 tsp paprika

1/4 tsp pepper

1/2 tsp salt

Directions:

Toss sliced radishes and onion with olive oil.

Spray air fryer basket with cooking spray.

Spray radish and onion mixture into the air fryer basket and cook at 360 F for 8 minutes.

Transfer radish and onion mixture into the mixing bowl. Add onion powder, garlic powder, paprika, pepper, and salt and toss well.

Return radish and onion mixture into the air fryer basket and cook for 5 minutes more.

Serve and enjoy.

Nutrition: Calories 125 Fat 7.4 g Carbohydrates 13.6 g Sugar 3.2 g Protein 3.6 g Cholesterol 0 mg

Breakfast Strata

Preparation Time: 6 hours

Cooking Time: 2 hours

Servings: 8

Ingredients:

18 eggs

2 packs of croutons

1 pack of cheddar

Salt & pepper

1 pack of chopped spinach

3 cups of milk

3 cups chopped ham

1 jar Red Peppers

Directions:

Preheat the Power XL Air Fryer Grill to 1350C or 2750F.

Spray the pan with a non-stick spray.

Spread layers of ham, spinach, cheese, and croutons, and red peppers.

Pour eggs mixed with milk and seasoning in the pan and refrigerate.

Bake for 2 hours and leave to rest for 15 minutes.

Nutrition: Calories: 140kcal, Carbs: 6g, Protein: 16g, Fat: 5g.

Scrambled Eggs Wonton Cups

Preparation Time: 15 minutes

Cooking Time: 10 minutes

Servings: 3

Ingredients:

6 wonton wrappers

6 eggs

3 Breakfast sausages

2 large peppers

4 mushrooms

3 onions

Butter

Salt and pepper to taste

Directions :

Preheat the Power XL Air Fryer Grill to 1770C or 3500F.

Make the scrambled eggs.

Fold the wrappers brushed with butter into the muffin pan

Mix the ingredients in a bowl and put it in the wrappers.

Bake for 10 minutes.

Nutrition: Calories: 130kcal, Carbs: 7g, Protein: 9g, Fat: 7g.

Sheet Pan Shakshuka

Preparation Time: 15 minutes

Cooking Time: 10 minutes

Servings: 4

Ingredients:

4 large eggs

1 large Anaheim chili, chopped

2 tbsp. vegetable oil

1/2 cup onion, chopped

1 tsp. cumin, ground

2 minced garlic cloves

1/2 cup feta cheese

1/2 tsp. paprika

1 can of tomatoes

Salt & pepper

Directions:

Sauté the chili and onions in vegetable oil until tender.

Pour in the remaining ingredients except for eggs and cook until thick.

Make 4 pockets to pour in the eggs.

Bake for 10 minutes at 1910C or 3750F in the Power XL Air Fryer Grill.

Top it off with feta.

Nutrition: Calories: 219kcal, Carbs: 20g, Protein: 10g, Fat: 11g.

Breakfast Casserole

Preparation Time:

Cooking Time: 40 minutes

Servings: 4

Ingredients:

3 tbsp. brown sugar

1/2 cup of flour

1/2 tsp. cinnamon powder

4 tbsp. margarine

2 tbsp. white sugar

For the Casserole

2 eggs

2-1/2 tbsp. white flour

1 tsp. baking powder

1 tsp. baking soda

2 tbsp. sugar

4 tbsp. margarine

1/2 cup of milk

1-1/3 cup of blueberries

1 tbsp. lemon zest

Directions:

Preheat the Power XL Air Fryer Grill by selecting the pizza/bake mode.

Adjust the temperature to 300°F

In a bowl, mix the casserole ingredients, then pour it into the Power XL Air Fryer Grill baking pan.

In a separate bowl, mix white sugar with flour, margarine, white sugar, and cinnamon.

Mix until a crumbly mixture is achieved, spread over the blueberry's mixture.

Transfer to the Power XL Air Fryer Grill and bake for 30 minutes

Serving Suggestions: Serve with a glass of juice

Nutrition: Calories: 101kcal, Fat: 9.4g, Carb: g0.3g, Proteins: 7g

Coconut-Blueberry Cereal

Preparation Time: 20 minutes

Cooking Time: 20 minutes

Servings: 4

Ingredients:

> 1/2 cup dried blueberries
>
> 1/2 cup unsweetened coconut flakes
>
> 1 cup pumpkin seeds
>
> 2 cups chopped pecans
>
> 6 medium dates, pitted
>
> 1/3 cup coconut oil
>
> 2 tsp. cinnamon
>
> 1/2 tsp. sea salt

Directions:

> Add coconut oil, dates and half the pecans to a food processor; pulse until finely ground.
>
> Add pumpkin seeds and the remaining pecans and continue pulsing until roughly chopped.
>
> Transfer the mixture to a large bowl and add cinnamon, vanilla and salt; spread on a baking sheet/ pan that can fit in your foodi air fry toaster oven and set on bake at 325

degrees for about 20 minutes or until browned.

Remove from the foodi air fry toaster oven and let cool slightly before stirring in blueberries and coconut.

Enjoy!

Nutrition: Calories: 372 kcal, Carbs: 12 g, Fat: 25.2 g, Protein: 20.1 g.

Air-Fried Omelet

Preparation Time:10 minutes

Cooking Time: 10 minutes

Servings: 2

Ingredients:

3 large eggs

100g ham, cut into small pieces

1/4 cup milk

3/4 cup mixed vegetables (mushrooms, scallions, bell pepper)

1/4 cup mixed cheddar and mozzarella cheese

1 tsp. mixed herbs

Salt and freshly ground pepper to taste

Directions:

Combine the eggs and milk in a medium bowl then add in the remaining Ingredients: apart from the cheese and mixed herbs and beat well using a fork.

Pour the egg mix into an evenly greased pan then place it in the basket of your air fry toaster oven.

Set on bake for 350 degrees for 10 minutes.

Sprinkle the cheese and mixed herbs on the
omelet halfway through Cooking Time.

Gently loosen the omelet from the sides of the
pan using a spatula.

Serve hot!

Nutrition: Calories: 278 kcal, Carbs: 1.3 g, Fat: 4.6
g, Protein: 24.1 g.

Sunny Side up Egg Tarts

Preparation Time: 15 minutes

Cooking Time: 20 minutes

Servings: 2

Ingredients:

4 eggs

3/4 cup shredded Gruyere cheese (or preferred cheese)

1 sheet of puff pastry

Minced chives for topping

Directions:

Start by flouring a clean surface then gently roll out your sheet of puff pastry and divide it into four equal squares.

If you have a small air fryer toast oven, start with two squares but if it's big enough, go ahead and place the squares on the basket and cook for about 8-10 minutes or until they turn golden brown.

Whilst still in the basket, gently make an indentation at the center of each square and sprinkle 2-4 tablespoons of shredded cheese in the well then crack an egg on top.

Cook for 5-10 minutes or to desired doneness. Remove from air fryer toast oven, sprinkle with chives and you are ready to eat!

Nutrition: Calories: 403 kcal, Carbs: 10.8 g, Fat: 29.4 g, Protein: 24.6 g.

Air Toasted Cheese Sandwich

Preparation Time: 15 minutes

Cooking Time: 20 minutes

Servings: 2

Ingredients:

2 eggs

4 slices of bread of choice

4 slices turkey

4 slices ham

6 tbsp. half and half cream

2 tsp. melted butter

4 slices Swiss cheese

1/4 tsp. pure vanilla extract

Powdered sugar and raspberry jam for serving

Directions:

Mix the eggs, vanilla and cream in a bowl and set aside.

Make a sandwich with the bread layered with cheese slice, turkey, ham, cheese slice and the top slice of bread to make two sandwiches. Gently press on the sandwiches to somewhat flatten them.

Spread out kitchen aluminum foil and cut it about the same size as the sandwich and spread the melted butter on the surface of the foil.

Dip the sandwich in the egg mixture and let it soak for about 20 seconds on each side. Repeat this for the other sandwich. Place the soaked sandwiches on the foil sheets then place on the basket in your fryer.

Set on toast and cook for 12 minutes then flip the sandwiches and brush with the remaining butter and cook for another 5 minutes or until well browned.

Place the cooked sandwiched on a plate and top with the powdered sugar and serve with a small bowl of raspberry jam.

Enjoy!

Nutrition: Calories: 735 kcal, Carbs: 13.4 g, Fat: 47.9 g, Protein: 40.8 g.

Crunchy Zucchini Hash Browns

Preparation Time: 30 minutes

Cooking Time: 15 minutes

Servings: 3

Ingredients:

4 medium zucchinis, peeled and grated

1 tsp. onion powder

1 tsp. garlic powder

2 tbsp. almond flour

1-1/2 tsp. chili flakes

Salt and freshly ground pepper to taste

2 tsp. olive oil

Directions:

Put the grated zucchini in between layers of kitchen towel and squeeze to drain excess water. Pour 1 teaspoon of oil in a pan, preferably non-stick, over medium heat and sauté the potatoes for about 3 minutes.

Transfer the zucchini to a shallow bowl and let cool. Sprinkle the zucchini with the remaining ingredients and mix until well combined.

Transfer the zucchini mix to a flat plate and pat it down to make 1 compact layer. Put in the fridge and let it sit for 20 minutes.

Set your air fryer toast oven to 360 degrees F.

Meanwhile take out the flattened zucchini and divide into equal portions using a knife or cookie cutter.

Lightly brush your air fryer toast oven's basket with the remaining teaspoon of olive oil.

Gently place the zucchini pieces into the greased basket and fry for 12-15 minutes, flipping the hash browns halfway through.

Enjoy hot!

Nutrition: Calories: 195 kcal, Carbs: 10.4 g, Fat: 13.1 g, Protein: 9.6 g.

Air Toasted French Toast

Preparation Time: 5 minutes

Cooking Time: 20 minutes

Servings: 3

Ingredients:

6 slices of preferred bread

3/4 cup of milk

3 eggs

1 tsp. pure vanilla extract

1 tbsp. ground cinnamon

Directions:

Combine all the Ingredients: apart from the bread in a medium bowl until well mixed.

Dunk each slice of bread into the egg mix, gently shake the excess off and place in a greased pan.

Air toast in the fryer, for 6 minutes.

To serve, drizzle with maple syrup.

Nutrition: Calories: 245 kcal, Carbs: 28.5 g, Fat: 7.5 g, Protein: 14.9 g.

Citrus Blueberry Breakfast Muffins

Preparation Time:15 minutes

Cooking Time: 15 minutes

Servings: 3-4

Ingredients:

2-1/2 cups cake flour

1/2 cup sugar

1/4 cup light cooking oil such as avocado oil

1/2 cup heavy cream

1 cup fresh blueberries

2 eggs

Zest and juice from 1 orange

1 tsp. pure vanilla extract

1 tsp. brown sugar for topping

Directions:

Start by combining the oil, heavy cream, eggs, orange juice and vanilla extract in a large bowl then set aside.

Separately combine the flour and sugar until evenly mixed then pour little by little into the wet ingredients.

Combine well unlit well blended but careful not to over mix.

Preheat your air fryer toast oven at 320 degrees F

Gently fold the blueberries into the batter and divide into cupcake holders, preferably, silicone cupcake holders as you won't have to grease them. Alternatively, you can use cupcake paper liners on any cupcake holders/ tray you could be having.

Sprinkle the tops with the brown sugar and pop the muffins in the fryer.

Bake for about 12 minutes. Use a toothpick to check for readiness. When the muffins have evenly browned and an inserted toothpick comes out clean, they are ready.

Take out the muffins and let cool.

Enjoy!

Nutrition: Calories: 289 kcal, Carbs: 12.8 g, Fat: 32 g, Protein: 21.1 g.

Peanut Butter and Jelly Breakfast Donuts

Preparation Time:15 minutes

Cooking Time: 12 minutes

Servings: 4

Ingredients:

For the Donuts:

1-1/4 cups all-purpose flour

1/2 tsp. baking soda

1/2 tsp. baking powder

1/3 cup sugar

1/2 cup buttermilk

1 large egg

1 tsp. pure vanilla extract

3 tbsp. unsalted, melted and divided into 2+1

3/4 tsp. salt

For the Glaze:

2 tbsp. milk

1/2 cup powdered sugar

2 tbsp. smooth peanut butter

Sea salt to taste

For the Filling:

1/2 cup strawberry or blueberry jelly

Directions:

Whisk together all the dry Ingredients: for the donut in a large bowl.

Separately combine the egg, buttermilk, melted butter and vanilla extract.

Create a small well at the center of the dry ingredients and pour in the egg mixture. Use a fork to combine the Ingredients: then finish off with a spatula.

Place the dough on a floured surface and knead the dough. It will start out sticky but as you knead, it's going to come together.

Roll out the dough to make a 3/4-inch-thick circle. Use a cookie cutter, or the top part of a cup to cut the dough into rounds.

Place the donuts on a parchment paper and then into your air fryer toast oven. You may have to cook in batches depending on the size of your air fryer toast oven.

Set on bagel for 12 minutes at 350 degrees F.

Use a pastry bag or squeeze bottle to fill the donuts with jelly.

Combine the glaze ingredients and drizzle on top of the donuts.

Enjoy!

Nutrition: Calories: 430 kcal, Carbs: 66.8 g, Fat: 14.6 g, Protein: 9.1 g.

French Toast

Preparation Time: 5 minutes

Cooking Time: 10 minutes

Servings: 4

Ingredients:

2 slices of bread

1 tsp. Liquid vanilla

3 eggs

1 tbsp. Margarine

Directions:

Preheat the Power XL Air Fryer Grill by setting it to toast/pizza mode.

Adjust the temperature to 375°F; insert the pizza tray.

In a bowl, whisk the eggs and vanilla

Spread the margarine on the bread, transfer into the egg and allow to soak

Place on the Power XL air fryer pizza rack and set Time to 6 minutes, flip after 3 minutes.

Serving Suggestions: Serve topped with yogurt and honey

Nutrition: Calories: 99kcal, Fat: 0.2g, Carb: 7g, Proteins: 5g

Raspberry Oatmeal

Preparation Time: 10 minutes

Cooking Time: 40 minutes

Servings: 4

Ingredients:

1 cups of shredded coconut

2 tsp. Stevia

1 tsp. Cinnamon powder

2 cups. Almond milk

1/2 cup of raspberries

Directions:

Mix all the ingredients in a bowl

Pour into the air fryer baking pan

Transfer to the Power XL Air Fryer Grill

Using the knob, select bake/pizza mode

Adjust the temperature to 360°F.

Bake for 15 minutes

Serve and enjoy

Serving Suggestions: Garnish with coconut

Nutrition: Calories: 172kcal, Fat: 5g, Carb: 5g, Proteins: 6g

Breakfast Egg and Tomatoes

Preparation Time:15 minutes

Cooking Time: 30 minutes

Servings: 2

Ingredients:

Salt and pepper to taste

2 eggs

2 large tomatoes

Directions:

Preheat the air fryer by selecting the bake/pizza mode.

Adjust the temperature to 375°F

Cut off the top of the tomatoes, scoop out the seed and flesh.

Break the egg into each tomato, transfer to the Power XL air fryer baking tray.

Bake for 24 minutes

Serve and enjoy

Serving Suggestions: garnish with chopped parsley

Nutrition: Calories: 95kcal, Fat: 5g, Carb: 5.5g, Proteins: 7g

Sausage Omelet

Preparation Time: 12 minutes

Cooking Time: 23 minutes

Servings: 2

Ingredients:

2 sausage, chopped

1 yellow onion

1 bacon slice

4 eggs

Directions:

Preheat the Power XL Air Fryer Grill by selecting air fry mode

Adjust temperature to 320°F and Time to 5 minutes

In a bowl, mix all the ingredients.

Pour into the air fryer baking tray

Transfer into the Power XL Air Fryer Grill

Air fry for 10 minutes

Serve and enjoy!

Serving Suggestions: Serve with toast bread

Directions: & Cooking Tips: add a handful of cheese to the egg mixture

Nutrition: Calories: 156kcal, Fat: 21g, Carb: 27g,

Proteins: 17g

Zucchini Fritters

Preparation Time:8 minutes

Cooking Time: 20 minutes

Servings: 4

Ingredients:

10 oz. zucchini

7 oz. halloumi cheese

2 eggs

1/4 cup all-purpose flour

1 tsp. dried dill

Salt and black pepper to taste

Directions:

Preheat the Power XL Air Fryer Grill by selecting bake/pizza mode

Adjust temperature to 360°F and Time to 5 minutes

In a bowl, mix all the ingredients.

Make small fritters from the mixture

Place them on the Air fryer baking tray

Transfer into the Power XL Air Fryer Grill

Bake for 7 minutes

Serve and enjoy!

Serving Suggestions: Serve with Vegetable salad

Nutrition: Calories: 170kcal, Fat: 15g, Carb: 7g, Proteins: 12g

Scrambled Egg

Preparation Time: 10 minutes

Cooking Time: 20 minutes

Servings: 1

Ingredients:

2 eggs

2 tbsp. Butter

1/4 cup of cheese

1 tomato

Directions:

Preheat the Power XL Air Fryer Grill by selecting air fry mode

Adjust temperature to 290°F and Time to 5 minutes

Grease the baking tray with the butter.

In a bowl, mix all the ingredients.

Pour into the Air fryer baking tray

Transfer into the Power XL Air Fryer Grill

Air fry for 7 minutes

Serving Suggestions: Serve with toast bread

Nutrition: Calories: 206kcal, Fat: 11.3g, Carb: 3g, Proteins: 12g

Sausage Wraps

Preparation Time: 10 minutes

Cooking Time: 20 minutes

Servings: 2

Ingredients:

1 cup. Mozzarella cheese

8 sausage

8 crescent rolled dough

Directions:

Preheat the Power XL Air Fryer Grill by selecting bake/ pizza mode

Adjust temperature to 380°F and Timer to 5 minutes

Open the dough, arrange cheese at one end of the dough

Add the sausage and roll, secure with a toothpick

Arrange the sausage wrap in the Air fryer baking tray

Transfer into the Power XL Air Fryer Grill

Bake for 7 minutes

Serve and enjoy

Serving Suggestions: serve with ketchup or BBQ sauce

Nutrition: Calories: 230kcal, Fat: 7g, Carb: 5g, Proteins: 10g

Bacon, Egg and Cheese Breakfast Hash

Preparation Time:15 minutes

Cooking Time: 35 minutes

Servings: 4

Ingredients:

2 slices of bacon

4 tiny potatoes

1/4 tomato

1 egg

1/4 cup of shredded cheese

Directions:

Preheat the Power XL Air Fryer Grill to 2000C or 4000F on bake mode. Set bits of bacon on a double-layer tin foil.

Cut the vegetables to place over the bacon. Crack an egg over it.

Shape the tin foil into a bowl and cook it in the Power XL Air Fryer Grill at 1770C or 3500F for 15-20 minutes. Put some shredded cheese on top.

Nutrition: Calories: 150.5 kcal, Carbs: 18g, Protein: 6g, Fat: 6g.

Maple Glazed Sausages and Figs

Preparation Time:10 minutes

Cooking Time: 40 minutes

Servings: 2

Ingredients:

2 tbsp. maple syrup

2 tbsp. balsamic vinegar

2 packages of (12 ounces each) fully cooked chicken, cooked garlic sausages

8 fully ripe fresh figs, cut lengthwise

1/2 large sweet onion, minced

1-1/2 lbs. Swiss chard, with sliced stems, minced leaves

2 tsp. olive oil

Salt and pepper

Directions:

Preheat the Power XL Air Fryer Grill to 2320C or 4500F, mix syrup with 1 tbsp. Vinegar in a tiny bowl. Put sausages with figs on a one-layer foil-lined oven tray.

Roast for 8-10 minutes by grazing the syrup mix throughout the cooking.

Cook the onions in the Power XL Air Fryer Grill in a bowl with wrapping for 9 minutes.

Mix oil and seasoning with 1 tsp. of vinegar.

Serve the chards with figs and sausages.

Nutrition: Calories: 450kcal, Carbs: 42g, Protein: 34g, Fat: 17g.

Bacon Brussels Sprouts

Preparation Time:10 minutes

Cooking Time: 30 minutes

Servings:4

Ingredient:

    1 lb. brussels sprouts, cut into half

    1/2 avocado, diced

    1/4 cup onion, sliced

    4 bacon slices, cut into pieces

    1 tsp garlic powder

    3 tbsp lemon juice

    2 tbsp balsamic vinegar

    3 tbsp olive oil

    Pepper

    Salt

Directions:

In a small bowl, whisk together oil, garlic powder, 2 tbsp lemon juice, and salt.

In a mixing bowl, toss brussels sprouts with 3 tablespoons of oil mixture.

Add brussels sprouts into the air fryer basket and cook at 370 F for 20 minutes. Toss halfway through.

Now top with bacon and onion and cook for 10 minutes more.

Transfer brussels sprouts mixture into the large bowl. Add basil, avocado, and remaining oil mixture, and lemon juice and toss well.

Serve and enjoy.

Nutrition: (Amount per Serving): Calories 248, Fat 16.5g, Carbohydrates 15.5g, Sugar 4.5g, Protein 11.7g, Cholesterol 21mg

Sausage Swiss Cheese Egg Bite

Preparation Time: 10 minutes

Cooking Time: 5 minutes

Servings: 7

Ingredients:

4 eggs

1 tbsp green onion, chopped

1/4 cup mushrooms, chopped

1/4 cup sausage, cooked and crumbled

1/2 cup cottage cheese, crumbled

1/2 cup Swiss cheese, shredded

Pepper

Salt

Directions:

Spray egg mold with cooking spray and set aside.

In a bowl, beat eggs until frothy. Add remaining Ingredients into the eggs and stir to mix.

Pour egg mixture into the egg mold.

Place egg mold into the air fryer basket and cook at 330 F for 5 minutes.

Serve and enjoy.

Nutrition: Calories 82, Fat 5.1g, Carbohydrates 1.3g, Sugar 0.4g, Protein 7.7g, Cholesterol 10 mg

Spicy Chicken Wings

Preparation Time: 10 minutes

Cooking Time: 25 minutes

Servings: 4

Ingredients:

2 lbs. chicken wings

1/2 tsp Worcestershire sauce

1/2 tsp Tabasco

6 tbsp butter, melted

12 oz hot sauce

Directions:

Spray air fryer basket with cooking spray.

Add chicken wings into the air fryer basket and cook at 380 F for 25 minutes. Shake basket after every 5 minutes.

Meanwhile, in a mixing bowl, mix together hot sauce, Worcestershire sauce, and melted butter. Set aside. Add chicken wings and toss well.

Serve and enjoy.

Nutrition: Calories 594, Fat 34.4g, Carbohydrates 1.6 g, Sugar 1.2g, Protein 66.2g, Cholesterol 248mg

Fajita Chicken

Preparation Time:10 minutes

Cooking Time: 17 minutes

Servings:4

Ingredients:

4 chicken breasts, make horizontal cuts on each piece

1/2 red bell pepper, sliced

2 tbsp fajita seasoning

1/2 green bell pepper, sliced

2 tbsp olive oil

1/2 cup cheddar cheese, shredded

1 onion, sliced

Pepper

Salt

Directions:

Line air fryer basket with aluminum foil.

Preheat the cosori air fryer to 380 F.

Rub oil and seasoning all over the chicken breast.

Place chicken into the air fryer basket and top with peppers and onion.

Cook for 15 minutes. Top with cheese and cook for 1-2 minutes more.

Serve and enjoy.

Nutrition: Calories 431, Fat 22.6 g, Carbohydrates 8.2 g, Sugar 2.7 g, Protein 46.4 g, Cholesterol 145 mg

Lemon Chicken Breasts

Preparation Time:10 minutes

Cooking Time: 20 minutes

Servings:4

Ingredients:

4 chicken breasts, skinless and boneless

1 preserved lemon

1 tbsp olive oil

Directions:

Add all Ingredients into the bowl and mix well.
Set aside for 10 minutes.

Spray air fryer basket with cooking spray.

Place chicken into the air fryer basket and cook
at 400 F for 20 minutes.

Serve and enjoy.

Nutrition: Calories 312, Fat 14.4 g, Carbohydrates
1.4 g, Sugar 0.4 g, Protein 42.4 g, Cholesterol 130
mg

Salmon Dill Patties

Preparation Time:10 minutes

Cooking Time: 10 minutes

Servings:2

Ingredients:

1 egg

14 oz salmon

1 tsp dill weed

1/2 cup almond flour

1/4 cup onion, diced

Pepper

Salt

Directions:

Line air fryer basket with parchment paper.

Add all Ingredients into the mixing bowl and mix until well combined.

Make patties from mixture and place into the air fryer basket.

Cook at 370 F for 10 minutes. Turn patties halfway through.

Serve and enjoy.

Nutrition: Calories 341, Fat 18 g, Carbohydrates 3.3 g, Sugar 1 g, Protein 43 g, Cholesterol 169 mg

Chicken Fritters

Preparation Time:10 minutes

Cooking Time: 10 minutes

Servings:4

Ingredients:

1 lb. ground chicken

1/2 tsp onion powder

1/2 tsp garlic powder

1/2 cup parmesan cheese, shredded

1/2 tbsp dill, chopped

1/2 cup almond flour

2 tbsp green onions, chopped

Pepper

Salt

Directions:

Line air fryer basket with parchment paper.

Add all Ingredients into the large bowl and mix until well combined.

Make patties from mixture and place into the air fryer basket.

Cook at 350 F for 10 minutes. Turn patties halfway through.

Serve and enjoy.

Nutrition: Calories 280, Fat 12.9 g, Carbohydrates 2.2 g, Sugar 0.4 g, Protein 37.8 g, Cholesterol 110 mg

Delicious Chicken Burger Patties

Preparation Time: 10 minutes

Cooking Time: 25 minutes

Servings: 5

Ingredients:

1 lb. ground chicken

1 egg, lightly beaten

1 cup Monterey jack cheese, grated

1 cup carrot, grated

1 cup cauliflower, grated

1/8 tsp red pepper flakes

2 garlic cloves, minced

1/2 cup onion, minced

3/4 cup almond flour

Pepper

Salt

Directions:

Line air fryer basket with parchment paper.

Add all Ingredients into the mixing bowl and mix until well combined.

Make patties from mixture and place into the air fryer basket.

71

Cook at 400 F for 25 minutes. Turn patties halfway through.

Serve and enjoy.

Nutrition: Calories 314, Fat 16.6 g, Carbohydrates 5.9 g, Sugar 2.4 g, Protein 34.6 g, Cholesterol 134 mg

Tuna Patties

Preparation Time: 10 minutes

Cooking Time: 10 minutes

Servings: 10

Ingredients:

15 oz can tuna, drained and flaked

1 celery stalk, chopped

3 tbsp parmesan cheese, grated

1/2 cup almond flour

1 tbsp lemon juice

2 eggs, lightly beaten

1/2 tsp dried herbs

1/2 tsp garlic powder

2 tbsp onion, minced

Pepper

Salt

Directions:

Line air fryer basket with parchment paper.

Add all Ingredients into the large bowl and mix until well combined.

Make patties from mixture and place into the air fryer basket in batches.

Cook at 360 F for 10 minutes. Turn patties halfway through.

Serve and enjoy.

Nutrition: Calories 86, Fat 2.9 g, Carbohydrates 0.9 g, Sugar 0.3 g, Protein 13.7 g, Cholesterol 49 mg

Sausage Cheese Breakfast Frittata

Preparation Time:10 minutes

Cooking Time: 10 minutes

Servings:2

Ingredients:

> 2 eggs
>
> 1 tbsp spring onions, chopped
>
> 1 breakfast sausage patty, chopped
>
> 1 tbsp butter, melted
>
> 2 tbsp cheddar cheese
>
> 1 tbsp bell peppers, chopped
>
> Pepper
>
> Salt

Directions:

> Spray air fryer safe pan with cooking spray and set aside.
>
> Add chopped sausage patty in pan and air fry at 350 F for 5 minutes.
>
> Meanwhile, in a bowl whisk together eggs, pepper, and salt. Add bell peppers, spring onions, and mix well.

Once sausages are cooked then pour the egg
mixture to the pan and mix well.

Sprinkle with cheese and air fry at 350 F for 5
minutes.

Serve and enjoy.

Nutrition: Calories 202 Fat 14.1 g Carbohydrates 6.7
g Sugar 3.5 g Protein 13 g Cholesterol 186 mg

Ham Egg Bites

Preparation Time:10 minutes

Cooking Time: 12 minutes

Servings:8

Ingredients:

6 eggs

1/2 cup cheddar cheese, shredded

1 cup ham, diced

2 tbsp cream

1/4 tsp garlic powder

1/4 tsp onion powder

Pepper

Salt

Directions:

In a bowl, whisk eggs with remaining ingredients.

Pour egg mixture into the silicone muffin molds.

Place molds into the air fryer basket and cook at 300 F for 12-14 minutes or until eggs are cooked.

Serve and enjoy.

Nutrition: Calories 106 Fat 7.2 g Carbohydrates 1.2

g Sugar 0.4 g Protein 8.8 g Cholesterol 140 mg

Pepperoni Omelet

Preparation Time: and Cooking Time: 25 minutes

Servings: 2

Ingredients:

2 tbsp. milk

4 eggs

10 pepperoni slices

Salt and ground black pepper to taste

Directions:

Preheat the Power XL Air Fryer Grill by selecting air fry mode.

Adjust temperature to 350°F and Time to five minutes.

In a bowl, mix all the ingredients.

Pour into the Air fryer baking tray.

Transfer into the Power XL Air Fryer Grill 6. Air fry for 12 minutes.

Serve and enjoy!

Nutrition: Calories: 456 Kcal, Fat: 32.9g, Carb: 6.2g, Protein: 22g

Pancetta and Hotdog Omelet

Preparation Time: and Cooking Time: 20 minutes

Servings: 2

Ingredients:

1 pancetta, chopped

1/4 tsp. dried rosemary

2 hot dogs, chopped

1/2 tsp. dried parsley

2 small onions, chopped

Directions:

In a bowl, crack the egg.

Add the remaining ingredients and mix, pour into the air fryer baking tray

Adjust temperature to 320°F

Set Time to 5 minutes

Open the door and arrange your baking pan

Air fry for 10 minutes

Serve and enjoy

Nutrition: Calories: 185kcal, Fat: 10.5g, Carb: 6g, Proteins: 15g

Cheese Garlic Quiche

Preparation Time:10 minutes

Cooking Time: 30 minutes

Servings:4

Ingredients:

6 eggs

1/2 cup onion, chopped

1/8 tsp cayenne

1/8 tsp nutmeg

8 oz cheddar cheese, grated

4 bacon slices, cooked and chopped

3/4 cup coconut milk

1/2 tsp garlic, minced

1 tbsp olive oil

Pepper

Salt

Directions:

Spray air fryer safe pan with cooking spray and set aside.

Heat oil in a pan over medium heat. Add onion and sauté for 5 minutes.

Add garlic and sauté for 30 seconds. Remove pan from heat and set aside to cool.

In a mixing bowl, whisk eggs with milk, pepper, and salt. Stir in sautéed onion garlic, cayenne, nutmeg, bacon, and cheese.

Pour egg mixture into the pan.

Place pan in the air fryer basket and cook at 350 F for 25 minutes.

Serve and enjoy.

Nutrition: Calories 566, Fat 47.6 g, Carbohydrates 5.5 g, Sugar 2.9 g, Protein 30.7 g, Cholesterol 326 mg

Easy Cheesy Breakfast Eggs

Preparation Time: 10 minutes

Cooking Time: 5 minutes

Servings: 1

Ingredients:

2 eggs

1 tsp parmesan cheese, grated

2 tbsp cheddar cheese, shredded

2 tbsp heavy cream

Pepper

Salt

Directions:

Spray ramekin dish with cooking spray and set aside.

In a small bowl, whisk eggs with parmesan cheese, cheddar cheese, heavy cream, pepper, and salt.

Pour egg mixture into the ramekin dish.

Place ramekin dish into the air fryer basket and cook at 330 F for 5 minutes.

Serve and enjoy.

Nutrition: Calories 332, Fat 27.5 g, Carbohydrates 2.3 g, Sugar 0.8 g, Protein 19.7 g, Cholesterol 393

mg

Cheesy Chicken Fritters

Preparation Time:10 minutes

Cooking Time: 25 minutes

Servings:4

Ingredients:

1 lb. ground chicken

3/4 cup almond flour

1 egg, lightly beaten

1 garlic clove, minced

1 1/2 cup mozzarella cheese, shredded

1/2 cup shallots, chopped

2 cups broccoli, chopped

Pepper

Salt

Directions:

Line air fryer basket with parchment paper.

Add all Ingredients into the mixing bowl and mix until well combined.

Make patties from mixture and place into the air fryer basket.

Cook at 390 F for 15 minutes. Turn patties and cook for 10 minutes more.

Serve and enjoy.

Nutrition: Calories 322, Fat 14.2 g, Carbohydrates 8.2 g, Sugar 1.1 g, Protein 40.1 g. Cholesterol 147 mg

Cheddar Cheese Omelet

Preparation Time:10 minutes

Cooking Time: 7 minutes

Servings:1

Ingredients:

> 3 eggs
>
> 1/2 tsp soy sauce
>
> 2 tbsp cheddar cheese, grated
>
> 1 onion, chopped
>
> 1/4 tsp garlic powder
>
> 1/4 tsp onion powder

Directions:

> Spray air fryer pan with cooking spray and set aside.
>
> In a bowl, whisk eggs with remaining ingredients. Pour egg mixture into the pan.
>
> Place pan in the air fryer basket and cook at 350 F for 6-7 minutes.

Nutrition: Calories 127. Fat 4.9 g, Carbohydrates 12.4 g, Sugar 4.5 g, Protein 9 g, Cholesterol 15 mg

Gruyere Cheese Egg Bite

Preparation Time:10 minutes

Cooking Time: 5 minutes

Servings:7

Ingredients:

4 eggs

1/4 cup bacon, cooked and crumbled

1/2 cup cottage cheese, crumbled

1/2 cup gruyere cheese, shredded

Directions:

Spray egg mold with cooking spray and set aside.

In a bowl, beat eggs until frothy. Add remaining Ingredients into the eggs and stir to mix.

Pour egg mixture into the egg mold.

Place egg mold into the air fryer basket and cook at 330 F for 5 minutes.

Nutrition: Calories 86 Fat 5.6 g Carbohydrates 0.8 g Sugar 0.3 g Protein 7.9 g Cholesterol 104 mg

Cheddar Cheese Broccoli Egg Bite

Preparation Time:10 minutes

Cooking Time: 5 minutes

Servings:7

Ingredients:

> 4 eggs
>
> 1/4 cup broccoli, cooked and chopped
>
> 1/2 cup cottage cheese, crumbled
>
> 1/2 cup cheddar cheese, shredded

Directions:

> Spray egg mold with cooking spray and set aside.
>
> In a bowl, beat eggs until frothy. Add remaining Ingredients into the eggs and stir to mix.
>
> Pour egg mixture into the egg mold.
>
> Place egg mold into the air fryer basket and cook at 330 F for 5 minutes.

Nutrition: Calories 84 Fat 5.5 g Carbohydrates 1.1 g Sugar 0.3 g Protein 7.5 g Cholesterol 103 mg

Cheese Sausage Pepper Frittata

Preparation Time:10 minutes

Cooking Time: 20 minutes

Servings:2

Ingredients:

- 4 eggs, lightly beaten
- 1 green onion, chopped
- 2 tbsp bell pepper, diced
- 1/2 cup Monterey jack cheese
- 1/4 lb. breakfast sausage, cooked and crumbled
- Pepper
- Salt

Directions:

Preheat the cosori air fryer to 360 F.

Spray air fryer pan with cooking spray and set aside.

In a bowl, whisk eggs with remaining ingredients. Pour egg mixture into the pan.

Place pan in the air fryer basket and cook for 18-20 minutes.

Serve and enjoy.

Nutrition: Calories 411 Fat 29.6 g Carbohydrates 10.7 g Sugar 7.2 g Protein 26.8 g Cholesterol 390 mg

Cottage Cheese Egg Cups

Preparation Time:10 minutes

Cooking Time: 15 minutes

Servings:6

Ingredients:

3 eggs, lightly beaten

2 tbsp green chilies, diced

2 tbsp cottage cheese

1 tbsp coconut milk

2 tbsp cheddar cheese, shredded

Pepper

Salt

Directions:

Spray egg mold with cooking spray and set aside.

In a bowl, whisk eggs with milk, pepper, and salt. Add cheddar cheese, green chilies, and cottage cheese and stir well.

Pour egg mixture in an egg mold.

Place egg mold into the air fryer basket and cook at 350 F for 15 minutes.

Serve and enjoy.

Nutrition: Calories 53 Fat 3.7 g Carbohydrates 1.1 g

Sugar 0.6 g Protein 4.2 g Cholesterol 85 mg

Cheese Mushroom Frittata

Preparation Time:10 minutes

Cooking Time: 6 minutes

Servings:2

Ingredients:

> 3 eggs
>
> 2 mushrooms, chopped
>
> 2 tbsp onion, chopped
>
> 1/4 bell pepper, diced
>
> 2 tbsp cheddar cheese, shredded
>
> 2 tbsp coconut milk
>
> Pepper
>
> Salt

Directions:

> Spray air fryer safe pan with cooking spray and set aside.
>
> In a bowl, whisk eggs with milk, pepper, and salt. Add remaining ingredients and stir well.
>
> Pour egg mixture into the pan
>
> Place pan in the air fryer basket and cook at 400 F for 6 minutes.
>
> Serve and enjoy.

Nutrition: Calories 170 Fat 12.6 g Carbohydrates 4.1 g Sugar 2.5 g Protein 11.2 g Cholesterol 253 mg

Cheese Omelet

Preparation Time:10 minutes

Cooking Time: 8 minutes

Servings:2

Ingredients:

2 eggs

1/4 cup cheddar cheese, shredded

1/4 cup heavy cream

Directions:

Spray air fryer safe pan with cooking spray and set aside.

In a bowl, whisk eggs with cream, pepper, and salt.

Pour egg mixture into the pan. Place pan in the air fryer basket and cook at 350 F for 4 minutes.

Sprinkle cheese on top and cook for 4 minutes more.

Nutrition: Calories 172 Fat 14.6 g Carbohydrates 1 g Sugar 0.4 g Protein 9.4 g Cholesterol 199 mg

Cheese Mushroom Egg Bake

Preparation Time:10 minutes

Cooking Time: 8 minutes

Servings:1

Ingredients:

2 eggs

1/2 cup ham, diced

1/4 cup cheddar cheese, shredded

1/4 cup coconut milk

2 mushrooms, sliced

1 tbsp green onion, chopped

Directions:

Spray air fryer safe pan with cooking spray and set aside.

In a bowl, whisk eggs with cheese, milk, pepper, and salt. Add ham, mushrooms, and green onion and stir well.

Pour egg mixture into the pan.

Place pan into the air fryer basket and cook at 330 F for 8 minutes.

Serve and enjoy.

Nutrition: Calories 498 Fat 38.3 g Carbohydrates 8.6

g Sugar 3.6 g Protein 31.9 g Cholesterol 396 mg

Cheese Egg Frittata

Preparation Time: 10 minutes

Cooking Time: 6 minutes

Servings: 2

Ingredients:

> 4 eggs
>
> 1/3 cup cheddar cheese, shredded
>
> 1/2 cup half and half
>
> Pepper
>
> Salt

Directions:

> Spray air fryer safe pan with cooking spray and set aside.
>
> In a small bowl, whisk eggs with cheese, half and half, pepper, and salt.
>
> Pour egg mixture into the pan.
>
> Place pan in the air fryer basket and cook at 320 F for 6 minutes.
>
> Serve and enjoy.

Nutrition: Calories 281 Fat 22 g Carbohydrates 3.6 g Sugar 0.9 g Protein 17.6 g Cholesterol 370 mg

Cheese Ham Egg Cups

Preparation Time:10 minutes

Cooking Time: 5 minutes

Servings:4

Ingredients:

4 eggs

1/2 cup cheddar cheese, shredded

4 tbsp heavy cream

1/2 cup ham, diced

Pepper

Salt

Directions:

Spray four ramekins with cooking spray and set aside.

In a small bowl, whisk eggs with cheese, heavy cream, ham, pepper, and salt.

Pour egg mixture into the ramekins.

Place ramekins into the air fryer basket and cook at 300 F for 5 minutes.

Serve and enjoy.

Nutrition: Calories 199 Fat 16.1 g Carbohydrates 1.6 g Sugar 0.4 g Protein 12.2 g Cholesterol 209 mg

Cheese Vegetable Frittata

Preparation Time:10 minutes

Cooking Time: 10 minutes

Servings:6

Ingredients:

4 eggs

3 tbsp heavy cream

1/2 cup cheddar cheese, shredded

1/4 cup leek, diced

1 cup spinach, diced

1 cup mushrooms, diced

Pepper

Salt

Directions:

Spray air fryer safe pan with cooking spray and set aside.

In a bowl, whisk together eggs, heavy cream, pepper, and salt.

Add cheese, leek, spinach, and mushrooms and stir well.

Pour egg mixture into the pan.

Place pan in the air fryer basket and cook at 300 F for 10 minutes.

Serve and enjoy.

Nutrition: Calories 112 Fat 8.9 g Carbohydrates 1.7 g Sugar 0.7 g Protein 6.8 g Cholesterol 129 mg

Cheesy Broccoli Bites

Preparation Time:15 m

Cooking Time 12 m

4 Servings

Ingredients:

2 cups broccoli florets

2 eggs, beaten

1¼ cups Cheddar cheese, grated

¼ cup Parmesan cheese, grated

1¼ cups breadcrumbs

Salt and freshly ground black pepper, to taste

Directions:

In a kitchen appliance, add the broccoli and pulse until finely chopped.

In an outsized bowl, add the chopped broccoli and remaining ingredients.

Make small equal-sized balls from the mixture.

Arrange the balls onto a baking sheet and refrigerate for at least a half-hour.

Turn the "Temperature Knob" of Power XL Air Fryer Grill to line the temperature to 360 degrees F.

Turn the "Function Knob" to settle on "Air Fry."

Turn the "Timer Knob" to line the Time for 12 minutes.

After preheating, arrange the balls in the air fryer basket in a single layer.

Insert the air fryer basket at position 2 of Air Fryer Grill.

When the cooking Time is over, transfer the balls onto a platter.

Serve warm.

Nutrition: Calories: 383 Kcal, Fat: 19.8g, Carb: 28g, Protein: 23g

Egg in a Hole

Preparation Time:5 Minutes

Cooking Time: 5 Minutes

Servings: 1

Ingredients:

One slice bread

One teaspoon butter softened

One egg

One tablespoon shredded Cheddar cheese

Two teaspoons diced ham

Directions:

Preheat the air fryer to 330ºF (166ºC). Place a baking dish in the air fryer basket.

On a flat surface, cut a hole in the bread slice's center with a 21/2-inch-diameter biscuit cutter.

Spread the butter lightly on each side of the bread slice and transfer to the baking dish.

Crack the egg into the hole, then season as desired with salt and pepper. Scatter the shredded cheese and diced ham on top.

Bake in the preheated air fryer for 5 minutes until the bread is lightly browned and the egg is cooked to your preference.

Remove from the basket and serve hot.

Nutrition: Calories: 243 Fat: 14.5g Carbs: 15.4g Protein: 12.6g

Simple Egg Souffle

Preparation Time:5 minutes

Cooking Time: 8 minutes

Servings: 2

Ingredients:

2 eggs

1/4 tsp chili pepper

2 tbsp heavy cream

1/4 tsp pepper

1 tbsp parsley, chopped

Directions:

In a bowl, whisk eggs with remaining gradients.

Spray two ramekins with cooking spray.

Pour egg mixture into the ramekins and place into the air fryer basket.

Cook soufflé at 390 F for 8 minutes

Nutrition: Calories 116 Fat 10 g Carbs 1.1 g Protein 6 g

Breakfast Scramble Casserole

Preparation Time: 20 minutes

Cooking Time: 10 minutes

Servings: 4

Ingredients:

6 slices bacon

6 eggs

Cooking oil

½ cup chopped red bell pepper

½ cup chopped green bell pepper

½ cup chopped onion

¾ cup shredded Cheddar cheese

Directions:

In a pan, over medium-high heat, cook the bacon, 5 to 7 minutes, flipping too evenly crisp. Dry out on paper towels, crumble, and set aside. In a medium bowl, whisk the eggs. Add salt and pepper to taste.

Spray a barrel pan with cooking oil. Make sure to cover the bottom and sides of the pan. Add the beaten eggs, crumbled bacon, red bell pepper, green bell pepper, and onion to the pan. Place the pan in the air fryer. Cook for 6 minutes Open the air fryer and sprinkle the cheese over the casserole. Cook for an additional 2 minutes.

Nutrition: Calories 116 Fat 10 g Carbs 1.1 g Protein 6 g

Cowboy Quiche

Preparation Time: 30 minutes

Cooking Time: 1 hour

Servings: 8

Ingredients:

　　1 red potato with sliced skin (keep it short)

　　1 onion, minced

　　1/2 jalapeno with minced seeds

　　1 stick butter, melted

　　10 white mushrooms, minced

　　5-7 bacon strips

　　1/2 cup of sliced ham

　　1/2 red pepper, minced

　　1/2 green pepper, minced

　　1/4 cup of grated Cheddar

　　1/4 cup of grated Gruyere

　　6 eggs

　　12 ounces milk

　　pint heavy cream

　　1 tsp. ground nutmeg

　　2 unbaked (9-inch) pie doughs

Directions:

Preheat the Power XL Air Fryer Grill to 1770C or 3500F. Put the veggies on a parchment paper-filled tray.

Put some melted butter with salt and pepper over vegetables, and bake for a quarter-hour.

Put mushrooms separately in a parchment paper-filled tray with melted butter on top. Cook for five minutes.

Cook bacon strips on a special tray until crisp.

Put minced ham inside the Power XL Air Fryer Grill and cook everything properly.

Mix all the Ingredients: to blend properly.

Stir eggs, milk, and cream separately, add some salt and black pepper with nutmeg and blend properly.

Add the ingredients in a pan containing raw crust with the egg mixture. Bake for 35 minutes.

Nutrition: Calories: 257.9kcal, Carbs: 24g, Protein: 11.6g, Fat: 9g

Scrambled Eggs

Preparation Time: 2 minutes

Cooking Time: 5 minutes

Servings: 2

Ingredients:

1/2 tbsp. unsalted butter

2 big eggs

1 tbsp. water kosher salt

Fresh ground pepper

Directions:

Turn the fan on for air circulation.

Put seasoned eggs on the lightly greased pan and canopy with foil.

Cook for 5-10 minutes or until the eggs are set

Use a spatula to stir the eggs and scrape the edges.

Nutrition: Calories: 149kcal, Carbs: 1g, Protein: 12g, Fat: 6.7g

Ingram Content Group UK Ltd.
Milton Keynes UK
UKHW050928170323
418346UK00033B/173

9 781803 179865